A
MEDITATIVE
COMMENTARY
ON THE
NEW TESTAMENT

THE LETTERS OF PETER, JOHN, AND JUDE: LIVING IN JESUS

A
MEDITATIVE
COMMENTARY
ON THE
NEW TESTAMENT

THE LETTERS OF PETER, JOHN, AND JUDE: LIVING IN JESUS

by Gary Holloway

LEAFWOOD
PUBLISHERS

THE LETTERS OF PETER, JOHN, AND JUDE:
Living In Jesus

Copyright 2008 by Gary Holloway

ISBN 978-0-89112-557-0

Printed in the United States of America

Cover design by Greg Jackson, Jackson Design Co., llc

For information contact:
Leafwood Publishers, Abilene, Texas
1-877-816-4455 toll free
www.leafwoodpublishers.com

08 09 10 11 12 13 / 7 6 5 4 3 2 1

To my dear friend, Phillip Camp, whom I love in the truth

C O N T E N T S

1 PETER: AT HOME WITH JESUS

2 PETER: THE COMING OF JESUS

THE LETTERS OF JOHN: JESUS AS LOVE

JUDE: DENYING JESUS

INTRODUCTION

HEARING GOD IN SCRIPTURE

Many good commentaries, guides, and workbooks exist on the various books of the Bible. How is this series different? It is not intended to answer all your scholarly questions about the Bible, or even make you an expert in the details of Scripture. Instead, this series is designed to help you hear the voice of God for your everyday life. It is a guide to meditation on the Bible, meditation that will allow the Bible to transform you.

We read in many ways. We might scan the newspaper for information, read a map for location, read a novel for pleasure, or read a textbook to pass a test. These are all good ways to read, depending on our circumstances.

A young soldier far away from home who receives a letter from his wife reads in yet another way. He might scan the letter quickly at first for news and information. But his longing for his beloved causes him to read the letter again and again, hearing her sweet voice in every line. He slowly treasures each word of this precious letter.

BIBLE STUDY

So also, there are many good ways to read the Bible, depending on our circumstances. Bible study is absolutely necessary for our life with God. We rightly study the Bible for information. We ask, "Who wrote this?" "When was it written?" "Who were the original readers?"

"How do these words apply to me?" More importantly, we want information about God. Who is he? What does he think of me? What does he want from me?

There is no substitute for this kind of close, dedicated Bible study. We must know what the Bible says to know our standing with God. We therefore read the Bible to discover true doctrine or teaching. But some in their emphasis on the authority and inspiration of the Bible have forgotten that Bible study is not an end in itself. We want to know God through Scripture. We want to have a relationship with the Teacher, not just the teachings.

Jesus tells some of God's people in his day, "You diligently study the Scriptures because you think that by them you possess eternal life. These are the Scriptures that testify about me, yet you refuse to come to me to have life" (John 5:39-40). He's not telling them to study their Bibles less, but he is reminding them of the deeper purpose of Bible study—to draw us to God through Jesus. Bible study is a means, not an end.

Yet the way many of us have learned to study the Bible may actually get in the way of hearing God. "Bible study" may sound a lot like schoolwork, and many of us were happy to get out of school. "Bible study" may call to mind pictures of intellectuals surrounded by books in Greek and Hebrew, pondering meanings too deep for ordinary people. The method of Bible study that has been popular for some time focuses on the strangeness of the Bible. It was written long ago, far away, and in languages we cannot read. There is a huge gap between us and the original readers of the Bible, a gap that can only be bridged by scholars, not by average folk.

There is some truth and some value in that "scholarly"method. It is true that the Bible was not written originally to us. Knowing ancient languages and customs can at times help us understand the Bible better. However, one unintended result of this approach is to make the Bible distant from the people of God. We may come to think that we can only hear God indirectly through Scripture, that his word must be filtered through scholars. We may even think that deep Bible study is a matter of mastering obscure information about the Bible.

MEDITATION

But we read the Bible for more than information. By studying it, we experience transformation, the mysterious process of God at work in us. Through his loving words, God is calling us to life with him. He is forming us into the image of his Son.

Reading the Bible is not like reading other books. We are not simply trying to learn information or master material. Instead, we want to stand under the authority of Scripture and let God master us. While we read the Bible, it reads us, opening the depths of our being to the overpowering love of God. "For the word of God is living and active. Sharper than any double-edged sword, it penetrates even to dividing soul and spirit, joints and marrow; it judges the thoughts and attitudes of the heart. Nothing in all creation is hidden from God's sight. Everything is uncovered and laid bare before the eyes of him to whom we must give account" (Hebrews 4:12-13).

Opening our hearts to the word of God is meditation. Although this way of reading the Bible may be new to some, it has a long heritage among God's people. The Psalmist joyously meditates on the words of God (Psalm 1:2; 39:3; 119:15, 23, 27, 48, 78, 97, 99, 148). Meditation is taking the words of Scripture to heart and letting them ask questions of us. It is slowing chewing over a text, listening closely, reading God's message of love to us over and over. This is not a simple, easy, or naïve reading of Scripture, but a process that takes time, dedication, and practice on our part.

There are many ways to meditate on the Bible. One is praying the Scriptures. Prayer and Bible study really cannot be separated. One way of praying the Bible is to make the words of a text your prayer.

Obviously, the prayer texts of Scripture, especially the Psalms, lend themselves to this. "The Lord is my shepherd" has been the prayer of many hearts.

However, it is proper and helpful to turn the words of the Bible into prayers. Commands from God can become prayers. "You shall have no other gods before me" (Exodus 20:3) can be prayed, "Lord, keep me from anything that takes your place in my heart." Stories can be prayed. Jesus heals a man born blind (John 9), and so we pray, "Lord Jesus open my eyes to who you truly are." Even the promises of the Bible become prayers. "Never will I leave you; never will I forsake you" (Deuteronomy 31:6; Hebrews 13:5) becomes "God help me know that you promise that you are always with me and so live my life without fear."

Obviously, there are many helpful ways of hearing the voice of God in Scripture. Again, the purpose of Bible reading and study is not to know more about the Bible, much less to pride ourselves as experts on Scripture. Instead, we read to hear the voice of our Beloved. We listen for a word of God for us.

HOLY READING

This commentary reflects one ancient way of meditation and praying the Scriptures known as *lectio divina* or holy reading. This method assumes that God wants to speak to us directly in the Bible, that the passage we are reading is God's word to us right now. The writers of the New Testament read the Old Testament with this same conviction. They saw the words of the Bible speaking directly to their own situation. They read with humility and with prayer.

The first step along this way of holy reading is listening to the Bible. Choose a biblical text that is not too long. This commentary breaks the letters of Peter, John, and Jude into smaller sections. The purpose is to hear God's voice in your current situation, not to cover material or prepare lessons. Get into a comfortable position and maintain silence before God for several minutes. This prepares the heart to listen. Read slowly. Savor each word. Perhaps read aloud. Listen for a particular phrase that speaks to you. Ask God, "What are you trying to tell me today?"

The next step is to meditate on that particular phrase. That meditation may include slowly repeating the phrase that seems to be for you today. As you think deeply on it, you might even memorize it. Committing biblical passages to memory allows us to hold them in our hearts all day long. If you keep a journal, you might write the passage there. Let those words sink deeply into your heart.

Then pray those words back to God in your heart. Those words may call up visual images, smells, sounds, and feelings. Pay attention to what God is giving you in those words. Then respond in faith to what those words say to your heart. What do they call you to be and to do? Our humble response might take the form of praise, thanksgiving, joy, confession, or even cries of pain.

The final step in this "holy reading" is contemplation of God. The words from God that we receive deeply in our hearts lead us to him. Through these words, we experience union with the all-powerful God of love. Again, one should not separate Bible reading from prayer. The words of God in Scripture transport us into the very presence of God where we joyfully rest in his love.

What keeps reading the Bible this way from becoming merely our own desires read back into Scripture? How do we know it is God's voice we hear and not our own?

Two things. One is prayer. We are asking God to open our hearts, minds, and lives to him. We ask to hear his voice, not ours and not the voice of the world around us.

The second thing that keeps this from being an exercise in self-deception is to study the Bible in community. By praying over

Scripture in a group, we hear God's word together. God speaks through the other members of our group. The wisdom he gives them keeps us from private, selfish, and unusual interpretations. They help us keep our own voices in check, as we desire to listen to God alone.

HOW TO USE THIS COMMENTARY

This commentary provides assistance in holy reading of the Bible. It gives structure to daily personal devotions, family meditation, small group Bible studies, and church classes.

DAILY DEVOTIONAL

Listening, meditation, prayer, contemplation. How does this commentary fit into this way of Bible study? Consider it as a conversation partner. We have taken a section of Scripture and then broken it down into four short daily readings. After listening, meditating, praying, and contemplating the passage for the day, use the questions suggested in the commentary to provoke deeper reflection. This provides a structure for a daily fifteen minute devotional four days a week. On the fifth day, read the entire passage, meditate, and then use the questions to reflect on the meaning of the whole. On day six, take our meditations on the passage as conversation with another who has prayed over the text.

If you want to begin daily Bible reading, but need guidance, this provides a Monday-Saturday experience that prepares the heart for worship and praise on Sunday. This structure also results in a communal reading of Scripture, instead of a private reading. Even if you use this commentary alone, you are not reading privately. God is at work in you and in the conversation you have with another (the author of the commentary) who has sought to hear God through this passage of the Bible.

FAMILY BIBLE STUDY

This commentary can also provide an arrangement for family Bible study. Many Christian parents want to lead their children in daily study, but don't know where to begin or how to structure their time. Using the six-day plan outlined above means the entire family can read, meditate, pray, and reflect on the shorter passages, using the questions provided. On day five, they can review the entire passage, and then on day six, read the meditations in the commentary to prompt reflection and discussion. God will bless our families beyond our imaginations through the prayerful study of his word.

WEEKLY GROUP STUDY

This commentary can also structure small group Bible study. Each member of the group should have meditated over the daily readings and questions for the five days preceding the group meeting, using the method outlined above. The day before the group meeting, each member should read and reflect on the meditations in the commentary on that passage. You then can meet once a week to hear God's word together. In that group meeting, the method of holy reading would look something like this:

Listening
1. Five minutes of silence.
2. Slow reading of the biblical passage for that week.
3. A minute of silent meditation on the passage.

4. Briefly share with the group the word or phrase that struck you.

Personal Message
5. A second reading of the same passage.
6. A minute of silence.
7. Where does this touch your life today?
8. Responses: I hear, I see, etc.

Life Response
9. Brief silence.
10. What does God want you to do today in light of this word?

Group Prayer
11. Have each member of the group pray aloud for the person on his or her left, asking God to bless the word he has given them.

The procedure suggested here can be used in churches or in neighborhood Bible studies. Church members would use the daily readings Monday-Friday in their daily devotionals. This commentary intentionally provides no readings on the sixth day, so that we can spend Saturdays as a time of rest, not rest from Bible study, but a time to let God's word quietly work its way deep into our hearts. Sunday during Bible school or in home meetings, the group would meet to experience the weekly readings together, using the group method described above. It might be that the sermon for each Sunday could be on the passage for that week.

Some churches have used this structure to great advantage. In the hallways of those church buildings, the talk is not of the local football team or the weather, but of the shared experience of the Word of God for that week.

And that is the purpose of our personal and communal study, to hear the voice of God, our loving Father who wants us to love him in return. He deeply desires a personal relationship with us. Father, Son, and Spirit make a home inside us (see John 14:16-17, 23). Our loving God speaks to his children! But we must listen for his voice. That listening is not a matter of gritting our teeth and trying harder to hear. Instead, it is part of our entire life with God. That is what Bible study is all about.

Through daily personal prayer and meditation on God's word and through a communal reading of Scripture, our most important conversation partner, the Holy Spirit, will do his mysterious and marvelous work. Among other things, the Spirit pours God's love into our hearts (Romans 5:5), bears witness to our spirits that we are God's children (Romans 8:16), intercedes for us with God (Romans 8:26), and enlightens us as to God's will (Ephesians 1:17).

So this is an invitation to personal daily Bible study, to praying the Scriptures, to sharing with fellow believers, to hear the voice of God. God will bless us, our families, our churches, and his world if we take the time to be still, listen, and do his word.

FIRST PETER: AT HOME WITH JESUS

THE SPIRITUALITY OF 1 PETER

This letter addresses Christians who are powerless by the world's standards, but who are greatly blessed by God. Their weak position in society should force them to rely more on the power of God through his Holy Spirit. In spite of facing trials—hostility from their bosses, neighbors, and even family—they are reminded of the great inheritance they have from God through the resurrection of Jesus. The spirituality of Peter is thus a working, on the ground, practical spirituality asking, "How can we live holy, victorious lives in a hostile culture?"

A Spirituality of Sanctification

Facing a threatening culture, Christians should rely on the Holy Spirit to make us holy. This "sanctifying work of the Spirit" (1 Peter 1:2), is central to the calling of God for our lives. Through the Spirit we experience the life of God himself. Thus God says to us his people, "Be holy, for I am holy." That holiness is not a withdrawal from the world or from other Christians. Since God has purified us, we must love our brothers and sisters deeply from the heart (1 Peter 1:22).

A Spiritual Temple

Indeed, our holiness makes us into priests for the sake of the world. As priests we offer spiritual sacrifices to God, that is, every aspect of our lives. Not only are we spiritual priests, but we are being built into a spiritual house, a holy temple in which the Spirit of God lives. Even the pagans who persecute us should see that our good actions glorify God. We live to praise him.

EVERYDAY LIFE IN THE SPIRIT

We live out our calling as God's holy priests and temple in the ordinary arenas of life. Thus Peter talks of our responsibility to government (and the limits of that responsibility). He urges us to submit even to harsh masters in the workplace. He encourages wives and husbands to be submissive and considerate, even to partners who are not Christian. As sanctified people who set apart Christ as Lord, we should be ready to give those around us a reason for the hope we have. Thus the work of the Spirit is not merely private and inward. That work reaches out in every relationship Christians experience.

THE SPIRIT AND SUFFERING

To follow Jesus is to suffer, not just the everyday trials that everyone experiences, but unfair treatment and punishment. Such injustice might lead us to despair. How can we be punished for doing right? But Peter reminds us that those fiery trails are not unusual. Christ also suffered. Instead, those trials are blessings, for they show that "the Spirit of glory and of God rests on you" (1 Peter 4:14).

So as we read this letter of 1 Peter, let us read it as Spirit-filled people. Although we may not face the same kinds of trials the original readers faced, we still need assurance through the Spirit that we are called by God. As we read, let us meditate on the ways that God has chosen us to live in our country, at our work, and as family.

STRANGERS HERE

(1 Peter 1:1-12)

Day One Reading and Questions

[1]Peter, an apostle of Jesus Christ,

To God's elect, strangers in the world, scattered throughout Pontus, Galatia, Cappadocia, Asia and Bithynia, [2]who have been chosen according to the foreknowledge of God the Father, through the sanctifying work of the Spirit, for obedience to Jesus Christ and sprinkling by his blood:

Grace and peace be yours in abundance.

1. *Think of some times when you felt like a stranger or a foreigner. Share that feeling with others. How are we strangers in the world as Christians?*

2. *What does it mean to be elect or chosen by God? How does that make us feel? What is the contrast in feeling between being chosen and being a stranger?*

3. *What does each member of the Trinity do for us in this passage? Should we talk more often of the Trinity—Father, Son, and Spirit?*

Day Two Reading and Questions

[3]Praise be to the God and Father of our Lord Jesus Christ! In his great mercy he has given us new birth into a living hope through the resurrection of Jesus Christ from the dead, [4]and into an inheritance that can never perish, spoil or fade—kept in heaven for you, [5]who through faith are shielded by God's power until the coming of the salvation that is ready to be revealed in the last time.

1. *What does the "new birth" mean to you?*

2. *What inheritance do we have as Christians? Why is it important that it cannot perish, spoil, or fade?*

3. *Why do we need to be shielded by God? How does this relate to being strangers in the world?*

Day Three Reading and Questions

[6]In this you greatly rejoice, though now for a little while you may have had to suffer grief in all kinds of trials. [7]These have come so that your faith—of greater worth than gold, which perishes even though refined by fire—may be proved genuine and may result in praise, glory and honor when Jesus Christ is revealed. [8]Though you have not seen him, you love him; and even though you do not see him now, you believe in him and are filled with an inexpressible and glorious joy, [9]for you are receiving the goal of your faith, the salvation of your souls.

1. *How can suffering be good news? Does this mean we desire suffering?*

2. *What are some ways we suffer now as Christians?*

3. *What does it mean that we are receiving salvation? Is salvation in the present or the future?*

Day Four Reading and Questions

[10]Concerning this salvation, the prophets, who spoke of the grace that was to come to you, searched intently and with the greatest care, [11]trying to find out the time and circumstances to which the Spirit of Christ in them was pointing when he predicted the sufferings of Christ and the glories that would follow. [12]It was revealed to them that they were not serving themselves but you, when they spoke of the things that have now been told you by those who have preached the gospel to you by the Holy Spirit sent from heaven. Even angels long to look into these things.

1. What does the Holy Spirit do in this passage?

2. What advantages do we have over the Old Testament prophets?

3. What advantages do we have over angels?

Day Five Reading and Questions

Go back and read the entire passage

1. What is the relationship between our future inheritance from God and our current situation in the world? Does the thought of eternity with God make this life more important or less important?

2. How can middle class American Christians relate to being strangers or foreigners in this world? Don't we fit in well with our culture?

3. What tries your faith?

MEDITATION ON 1 PETER 1:1-12

I've come to mostly like this world. Most days, life is sweet. I'm warm in the winter and cool in the summer. I have a house, food, and a retirement program. I usually like my job. I have family and friends who love me. I have a church that appreciates me.

I don't think I am alone. There are many of us who can't complain (although we still do).

So how can we hear the message of Peter? How can we listen to words about homelessness and trials? How can we feel like strangers when we are so at home in the world?

Perhaps we need to return to the story of Jesus. The one who made the world was rejected by the world. He had nowhere to lay his head. He had no bank account or retirement. Although some admired him, eventually they turned on him and put him to death. Death on a cross. Death for a criminal. Death for a loser. Jesus was a stranger in his own world, his own nation, his own town, his own family.

Maybe we do not feel like strangers because we do not follow Jesus. We claim to, but we want both Jesus and the comforts of this world.

For those who are strangers and homeless, Peter's words are a comfort in their trials. Those trials create character. That suffering is not forever. Strangers here, we have a home with God that no one can take away.

For those of us who are too much at home in the world, his words are a call to repentance. Let us place our hope in God alone. Let us, like Jesus, trust God for life, for comfort, for success. Let us give up our treasure here so we can claim that sure inheritance, that great salvation that prophets and angels long to look into.

"Father we confess we are too much at home here. Lord Jesus, we have not always followed you into poverty, trial, and cross. Forgive!"

AT HOME WITH GOD

(1 Peter 1:13-25)

DAY ONE READING AND QUESTIONS

¹³Therefore, prepare your minds for action; be self-controlled; set your hope fully on the grace to be given you when Jesus Christ is revealed. ¹⁴As obedient children, do not conform to the evil desires you had when you lived in ignorance. ¹⁵But just as he who called you is holy, so be holy in all you do; ¹⁶for it is written: "Be holy, because I am holy."

1. *In what ways do we need to prepare our minds, to "lace up our shoes" to serve God?*

2. *Do we truly rely on God for self-control or rely on our own power? What specific areas are challenges to your self-control? Can God help you there?*

3. *What is your first reaction to the word, "holy"? Why? What does it mean to be holy?*

DAY TWO READING AND QUESTIONS

¹⁷Since you call on a Father who judges each man's work impartially, live your lives as strangers here in reverent fear. ¹⁸For you know that it was not with perishable things such as silver or gold that you were redeemed from the empty way of life handed down to you from your forefathers, ¹⁹but with the precious blood of Christ, a lamb

without blemish or defect. [20]He was chosen before the creation of the world, but was revealed in these last times for your sake. [21]Through him you believe in God, who raised him from the dead and glorified him, and so your faith and hope are in God.

1. *What is the difference between being afraid of God and having reverent fear of him?*

2. *How was our way of life empty before we became Christians?*

3. *What redeems us from that empty life? What does this say about our value in the eyes of God?*

Day Three Reading and Questions

[22]Now that you have purified yourselves by obeying the truth so that you have sincere love for your brothers, love one another deeply, from the heart.

1. *Why should we love those brothers and sisters in Christ who are particularly unlovable?*

2. *Why should we obey God?*

3. *What does it mean to purify oneself? How does this relate to holiness?*

Day Four Reading and Questions

[23]For you have been born again, not of perishable seed, but of imperishable, through the living and enduring word of God. [24]For,
"All men are like grass,
and all their glory is like the flowers of the field;
the grass withers and the flowers fall,

²⁵but the word of the Lord stands forever." And this is the word that was preached to you.

1. How does being born again relate to being holy? To loving our brothers and sisters?

2. How are we like grass? Why do we need this reminder?

3. Why is it encouraging that the word of the Lord stands forever?

DAY FIVE READING AND QUESTIONS

Go back and read the entire passage.

1. How does setting our hope on the Second Coming help us to be holy?

2. Why is it important that God is an impartial judge?

3. Should Christians actively pursue holiness or allow God to make us holy through his Spirit? Is Christianity mainly active or passive?

MEDITATION ON 1 PETER 1:13-25

Life is short and then you die. A cliché, but true.
The Bible puts it this way, "People are like grass that fades away."
Life is not only short, but often empty.
But we have been given full lives, meaningful lives, eternal lives, through the precious blood of Christ.
So how do we live? What does a redeemed life look like?
It is a holy life. Unfortunately "holy" has lost most of its meaning in our time. We cannot hear the word without thinking of religious pretenders who act as if they are better than others. But true holiness is belonging to God. It means sharing in his character—his genuine

goodness, unbounded love, and indescribable joy. Redeemed, born-again people are not focused on their own desires but on God. They genuinely care for others. Their lives are pure, rich, and full.

Although we are strangers in our own land, God makes a home for us with him. God gives us life. We may be like grass, but we are God's grass, God's field, God's garden. He makes our lives fruitful. In him we bloom and grow into holiness.

"Father, make us holy. Lord Jesus, you have bought us with your blood. Give us life! Fill us with your love! Reveal yourself fully to us so we may have your grace!"

GROWING UP IN GOD'S HOME

(1 Peter 2:1-25)

DAY ONE READING AND QUESTIONS

[1]Therefore, rid yourselves of all malice and all deceit, hypocrisy, envy, and slander of every kind. [2]Like newborn babies, crave pure spiritual milk, so that by it you may grow up in your salvation, [3]now that you have tasted that the Lord is good.

[4]As you come to him, the living Stone—rejected by men but chosen by God and precious to him—[5]you also, like living stones, are being built into a spiritual house to be a holy priesthood, offering spiritual sacrifices acceptable to God through Jesus Christ. [6]For in Scripture it says:

"See, I lay a stone in Zion,
    a chosen and precious cornerstone,
and the one who trusts in him
    will never be put to shame."

[7]Now to you who believe, this stone is precious. But to those who do not believe,

"The stone the builders rejected
    has become the capstone," [8]and,

"A stone that causes men to stumble
    and a rock that makes them fall." They stumble because they disobey the message—which is also what they were destined for.

1. What is the pure spiritual milk we should crave? Do we crave it?

2. What kind of sacrifices should we offer to God? If Jesus is our sacrifice, why do we need to offer other sacrifices?

3. Why do some people reject Jesus? Do they always realize they are rejecting him?

DAY TWO READING AND QUESTIONS

[9]But you are a chosen people, a royal priesthood, a holy nation, a people belonging to God, that you may declare the praises of him who called you out of darkness into his wonderful light. [10]Once you were not a people, but now you are the people of God; once you had not received mercy, but now you have received mercy.

[11]Dear friends, I urge you, as aliens and strangers in the world, to abstain from sinful desires, which war against your soul. [12]Live such good lives among the pagans that, though they accuse you of doing wrong, they may see your good deeds and glorify God on the day he visits us.

1. What does it mean to be priests to others?

2. Is praise the primary purpose of the church? If not, why not?

3. Think about the last time someone reacted angrily to you because you were a Christian. Why did they react this way? Were they justified? How did you react?

DAY THREE READING AND QUESTIONS

[13]Submit yourselves for the Lord's sake to every authority instituted among men: whether to the king, as the supreme authority, [14]or

to governors, who are sent by him to punish those who do wrong and to commend those who do right. [15]For it is God's will that by doing good you should silence the ignorant talk of foolish men. [16]Live as free men, but do not use your freedom as a cover-up for evil; live as servants of God. [17]Show proper respect to everyone: Love the brotherhood of believers, fear God, honor the king.

[18]Slaves, submit yourselves to your masters with all respect, not only to those who are good and considerate, but also to those who are harsh.

1. When should we refuse to submit to the government?

2. How does living right silence the talk of the ignorant?

3. If you hate your job and feel like a slave, what should you do?

Day Four Reading and Questions

[19]For it is commendable if a man bears up under the pain of unjust suffering because he is conscious of God. [20]But how is it to your credit if you receive a beating for doing wrong and endure it? But if you suffer for doing good and you endure it, this is commendable before God. [21]To this you were called, because Christ suffered for you, leaving you an example, that you should follow in his steps.

[22]"He committed no sin,
   and no deceit was found in his mouth."

[23]When they hurled their insults at him, he did not retaliate; when he suffered, he made no threats. Instead, he entrusted himself to him who judges justly. [24]He himself bore our sins in his body on the tree, so that we might die to sins and live for righteousness; by his wounds you have been healed. [25]For you were like sheep going astray, but now you have returned to the Shepherd and Overseer of your souls.

1. Specifically, how are we to follow in the steps of Jesus, according to this passage?

2. Why didn't Jesus retaliate against those who unjustly crucified him?

3. What do shepherd and overseer mean to you?

DAY FIVE READING AND QUESTIONS

Go back and read the entire passage.

1. Explain the "stone" illustration.

2. Is suffering the "normal state" for Christians.

3. How can we follow the "golden rule" when it goes so much against our nature?

MEDITATION ON 1 PETER 2:1-25

From stranger to chosen. What a great transformation!

We know what it feels like to be a stranger. As an outsider we do not belong. We do not fit in. Others think us strange and we feel strange. It is a lonely thing to be a stranger, an exile, a refugee.

But it's wonderful to be chosen. Someone or some group singles us out and says, "You belong to us." It is most wonderful to be chosen by God. "A chosen people, a royal priesthood, a holy nation, a people belonging to God." That's who we are!

What does it mean to belong to God? It means confidence and contentment. It means purpose and priesthood. It means holiness and honor.

It also means suffering. The more we act as those who belong to God, the more strange we are to the world. The world hates strangers. As God's people we freely submit to human authorities but we are not surprised when those authorities turn against us as illegal aliens. We are not even surprised when some respond to our love with hatred. That's what they did with Jesus. To belong to God means we suffer with Jesus, the great Shepherd of our lives. It means we suffer like Jesus—without retaliation, returning good for evil.

We do not belong to the world. We belong to Jesus. And so we live holy, peaceful, free, and suffering lives. But by his wounds ours are healed.

"Loving God, you have made us your own. We belong to you. Faithful Shepherd, you have healed us and shown us how to suffer. May we live this day as your holy people."

GOD'S FAMILY
(1 Peter 3:1-22)

DAY ONE READING AND QUESTIONS

[1]Wives, in the same way be submissive to your husbands so that, if any of them do not believe the word, they may be won over without words by the behavior of their wives, [2]when they see the purity and reverence of your lives. [3]Your beauty should not come from outward adornment, such as braided hair and the wearing of gold jewelry and fine clothes. [4]Instead, it should be that of your inner self, the unfading beauty of a gentle and quiet spirit, which is of great worth in God's sight. [5]For this is the way the holy women of the past who put their hope in God used to make themselves beautiful. They were submissive to their own husbands, [6]like Sarah, who obeyed Abraham and called him her master. You are her daughters if you do what is right and do not give way to fear.

1. *Name some godly women who showed Jesus to you. How did they do it?*

2. *What is your first reaction to the word, "submission"? What does it mean to submit? Is it unrealistic to expect submission in our society?*

3. *In what ways does our culture promote a false sense of beauty?*

Day Two Reading and Questions

[7]Husbands, in the same way be considerate as you live with your wives, and treat them with respect as the weaker partner and as heirs with you of the gracious gift of life, so that nothing will hinder your prayers.

[8]Finally, all of you, live in harmony with one another; be sympathetic, love as brothers, be compassionate and humble. [9]Do not repay evil with evil or insult with insult, but with blessing, because to this you were called so that you may inherit a blessing. [10]For,

"Whoever would love life
 and see good days
must keep his tongue from evil
 and his lips from deceitful speech.
[11]He must turn from evil and do good;
 he must seek peace and pursue it.
[12]For the eyes of the Lord are on the righteous
 and his ears are attentive to their prayer,
but the face of the Lord is against those who do evil."

1. Why do some men abuse their wives?

2. In what way are wives weaker? Does this imply they are inferior?

3. What makes a wife truly beautiful? What makes a husband truly strong?

Day Three Reading and Questions

[13]Who is going to harm you if you are eager to do good? [14]But even if you should suffer for what is right, you are blessed. "Do not fear what they fear; do not be frightened." [15]But in your hearts set apart Christ as Lord. Always be prepared to give an answer to everyone who asks you to give the reason for the hope that you have.

But do this with gentleness and respect, [16]keeping a clear conscience, so that those who speak maliciously against your good behavior in Christ may be ashamed of their slander. [17]It is better, if it is God's will, to suffer for doing good than for doing evil.

1. *What questions have others asked you concerning your hope in Christ? How did you answer?*

2. *When people laugh at us or look down on us because of our Christian beliefs, what is our first reaction? Is that the proper Christian response?*

3. *If people don't like us and treat us badly, is that a certain sign that we are faithful Christians? Why not?*

Day Four Reading and Questions

[18]For Christ died for sins once for all, the righteous for the unrighteous, to bring you to God. He was put to death in the body but made alive by the Spirit, [19]through whom also he went and preached to the spirits in prison [20]who disobeyed long ago when God waited patiently in the days of Noah while the ark was being built. In it only a few people, eight in all, were saved through water, [21]and this water symbolizes baptism that now saves you also—not the removal of dirt from the body but the pledge of a good conscience toward God. It saves you by the resurrection of Jesus Christ, [22]who has gone into heaven and is at God's right hand—with angels, authorities and powers in submission to him.

1. *What does it mean that Jesus preached to the spirits in prison? Do the dead get the gospel preached to them?*

2. *Some translations say baptism is an appeal to God for a good conscience. Is baptism a prayer? If so, how?*

3. According to Peter, how does baptism save us?

DAY FIVE READING AND QUESTIONS

Go back and read the entire passage.

1. Do you think physical persecution of Christians will ever occur in America?

2. Does fear of persecution keep us from being prepared to give answers concerning our hope?

3. List all the ways prayer is described in this passage.

MEDITATION ON 1 PETER 3:1-22

It's great to be part of the family of God. But what does it mean?

It means living a submissive life. But submission does not come naturally. Submission may even sound like cowardice. If we submit to abusive husbands or to anyone who harms us for doing good, are we not enabling their evil behavior? Should we not take a stand against abuse?

Of course we should. But we stand against evil as Jesus did. That's what it means to be part of God's family. And how did Jesus stand against evil? Not through violence, but through sacrifice.

Therefore, to live in God's family means we give ourselves for our own families. Wives live pure and reverent lives in front of their husbands and children. Husbands show consideration to their wives. We all live in harmony with others. Even when unfairly abused, we show love and forgiveness to those who harm us. That's the way of Jesus. That's the family we entered at baptism.

And we live in that family through prayer. We treat wives and husbands with gentleness so nothing hinders our prayers. We bless those who abuse us. We share our hope with those who wonder about the difference in our lives.

We may be strangers here, but we are at home with God, the God who became flesh and gave himself for us.

"Loving Father, through the power of Jesus, move us to forgive our enemies, especially those of our own families who harm us. Teach us what it means to be part of your family."

SUFFERERING WITH JESUS

(1 Peter 4:1-19)

DAY ONE READING AND QUESTIONS

[1]Therefore, since Christ suffered in his body, arm yourselves also with the same attitude, because he who has suffered in his body is done with sin. [2]As a result, he does not live the rest of his earthly life for evil human desires, but rather for the will of God. [3]For you have spent enough time in the past doing what pagans choose to do—living in debauchery, lust, drunkenness, orgies, carousing and detestable idolatry. [4]They think it strange that you do not plunge with them into the same flood of dissipation, and they heap abuse on you. [5]But they will have to give account to him who is ready to judge the living and the dead. [6]For this is the reason the gospel was preached even to those who are now dead, so that they might be judged according to men in regard to the body, but live according to God in regard to the spirit.

1. *How does suffering help us in our struggle with sin?*

2. *Have you ever been abused because you would not join others in sin? How did that make you feel? How did you react?*

3. *Why does this passage mention judgment? Is this meant to frighten us or encourage us? Who will be judged?*

DAY TWO READING AND QUESTIONS

[7]The end of all things is near. Therefore be clear minded and self-controlled so that you can pray. [8]Above all, love each other deeply, because love covers over a multitude of sins. [9]Offer hospitality to one another without grumbling. [10]Each one should use whatever gift he has received to serve others, faithfully administering God's grace in its various forms. [11]If anyone speaks, he should do it as one speaking the very words of God. If anyone serves, he should do it with the strength God provides, so that in all things God may be praised through Jesus Christ. To him be the glory and the power for ever and ever. Amen.

1. "The end is near." Is this good news or bad news?

2. How are love and forgiveness a comfort in suffering?

3. Do you hear the word of God in most sermons and Bible lessons you hear? What prevents us from hearing God there?

DAY THREE READING AND QUESTIONS

[12]Dear friends, do not be surprised at the painful trial you are suffering, as though something strange were happening to you. [13]But rejoice that you participate in the sufferings of Christ, so that you may be overjoyed when his glory is revealed. [14]If you are insulted because of the name of Christ, you are blessed, for the Spirit of glory and of God rests on you.

1. Why might we be surprised at suffering? Is unfair suffering always surprising?

2. Is participating in the sufferings of Christ the same thing as taking up the cross?

3. What is the sign of the presence of the Spirit in this passage?

Day Four Reading and Questions

[15]If you suffer, it should not be as a murderer or thief or any other kind of criminal, or even as a meddler. [16]However, if you suffer as a Christian, do not be ashamed, but praise God that you bear that name. [17]For it is time for judgment to begin with the family of God; and if it begins with us, what will the outcome be for those who do not obey the gospel of God? [18]And,

"If it is hard for the righteous to be saved,
what will become of the ungodly and the sinner?"

[19]So then, those who suffer according to God's will should commit themselves to their faithful Creator and continue to do good.

1. What is a meddler? Are we more tempted to meddle than to kill or steal? Why might meddlers suffer?

2. Why might we be tempted to be ashamed when we suffer as Christians?

3. What two things should Christians that suffer do? How are these two things related?

Day Five Reading and Questions

Go back and read the entire passage.

1. Persecution seems so far removed from our experience. Should we suffer more than we do as Christians? Why don't we suffer more?

2. Isn't the gospel good news? Then why all this talk of suffering? Shouldn't we draw others to Jesus by showing the good he does them? Doesn't talk of suffering get in the way of evangelism?

3. Why did Jesus have to suffer?

MEDITATION ON 1 PETER 4:1-19

I am willing to face the consequences of my actions. I am willing to experience loss, failure, and harsh treatment if I have them coming to me.

Not.

In truth, I'd rather avoid the trouble I deserve. But what really makes me angry is when people turn against me for trying to help them. There is no hurt deeper than unfair treatment.

Have you ever received a speeding ticket unfairly? Have you ever been cheated by a business? By the government? By a friend? How did you feel?

Yet Peter tells us that when we follow Jesus we will suffer unjustly. But that isn't fair! No. it's not. It was not fair for Jesus to be crucified for the very people who put him on the cross. It was not fair for the one who is Love Himself to be spat upon, beaten, and rejected.

Peter tells us, "Dear friends, do not be surprised at the painful trial you are suffering, as though something strange were happening to you." But it does feel strange to be hurt by the very people we are trying to help. Have you ever gone out of your way to feed the homeless, only to become a victim of their violence? Have you ever defended a friend in front of others, only to have her stab you in the back? Have you quietly given generous sums to a charity, only to have someone call you greedy?

It hurts. It's not fair. It is the way of Jesus.

Don't be surprised, but rejoice.

"Lord Jesus, we want to be like you. But we do not want to suffer. Give us the same trust you had, trust in a God who will make all things right."

LEADERS AGAINST THE ENEMY

(1 Peter 5:1-14)

DAY ONE READING AND QUESTIONS

¹To the elders among you, I appeal as a fellow elder, a witness of Christ's sufferings and one who also will share in the glory to be revealed: ²Be shepherds of God's flock that is under your care, serving as overseers—not because you must, but because you are willing, as God wants you to be; not greedy for money, but eager to serve; ³not lording it over those entrusted to you, but being examples to the flock. ⁴And when the Chief Shepherd appears, you will receive the crown of glory that will never fade away.

1. *What do the three terms for leaders in this passage—elder, shepherd, and overseer—say about their role?*

2. *What does it mean to lead out of compulsion? Why is this bad for a church?*

3. *Have you ever been in a congregation with "lordly" leaders? What can be done to prevent such leadership?*

DAY TWO READING AND QUESTIONS

⁵Young men, in the same way be submissive to those who are older. All of you, clothe yourselves with humility toward one another, because,

"God opposes the proud
   but gives grace to the humble."

⁶Humble yourselves, therefore, under God's mighty hand, that he may lift you up in due time. ⁷Cast all your anxiety on him because he cares for you.

1. *How is humility necessary for good leadership? For good followship?*

2. *How are humility and submission related? Does our society prize these virtues?*

3. *Why might humility and submission lead to anxiety? What should we do with our worries?*

Day Three Reading and Questions

⁸Be self-controlled and alert. Your enemy the devil prowls around like a roaring lion looking for someone to devour. ⁹Resist him, standing firm in the faith, because you know that your brothers throughout the world are undergoing the same kind of sufferings.

1. *What are ways we sleep in the face of danger from our enemy the devil?*

2. *Do Christians today talk too much or too little about the devil? Why?*

3. *How does knowing that others are suffering help us stand firm in the faith?*

Day Four Reading and Questions

¹⁰And the God of all grace, who called you to his eternal glory in Christ, after you have suffered a little while, will himself restore you and make you strong, firm and steadfast. ¹¹To him be the power for ever and ever. Amen.

[12]With the help of Silas, whom I regard as a faithful brother, I have written to you briefly, encouraging you and testifying that this is the true grace of God. Stand fast in it. [13]She who is in Babylon, chosen together with you, sends you her greetings, and so does my son Mark. [14]Greet one another with a kiss of love.

Peace to all of you who are in Christ.

1. What does "eternal glory" mean to you? Does it seem real or is it just a fond wish?

2. What are some ways God has "restored" you?

3. How do we stand fast in the true grace of God? What leads us away from grace?

DAY FIVE READING AND QUESTIONS

Go back and read the entire passage.

1. Throughout the Bible, Babylon was the place of exile and punishment for God's people. What city was "Babylon" in Peter's day? In what ways do we live in "Babylon" today?

2. How are good leadership and resisting the devil related?

3. Peter writes to encourage. How is all the talk of suffering in this letter encouraging talk?

MEDITATION ON 1 PETER 5:1-14

It's hard to be leader.

A leader risks loneliness and misunderstanding. A leader faces opposition and burn-out. A leader often sees nothing but problems and crises.

It's even harder to be a leader like Jesus. For Jesus will not let us be the boss, "lording it over" those we lead. Jesus instead calls us to be shepherds who tenderly watch over and care for the flock. He calls for firm gentleness. He draws us into his life of sacrificial service. He is the Great Shepherd.

It's hard to be a follower. Especially if we tend to be rebels, thinking our ideas are almost always better than those who lead us. It is even harder to follow like Jesus—to be humble, obedient, and accepting of authority. But we must humble ourselves under God's mighty power, a power sometimes seen through human leaders.

It's hard to pay attention. To be aware. To stay alert. Alert to the enemy. Aware of those who suffer. Paying attention to the kindness of God.

Lead! Follow! Wake-up! These are the words of encouragement we need. More than any other, we need this final encouragement, "Stand firm in God's grace."

"God of love, keep me firm in your grace. Teach me to lead, to follow, and to pay attention."

2 PETER: THE COMING OF JESUS

THE SPIRITUALITY OF 2 PETER

This short letter mentions the Holy Spirit only once, but reflects his work throughout. While the letter warns against specific false teachings and misunderstandings, it does so in a context of wholesome thinking and living, prompted by the power of God.

SHARING IN GOD'S NATURE

Although not attributed directly to the Holy Spirit, the letter speaks of the divine power that gives us all we need for a holy living (2 Peter 1:3). That power allows us to be participants in the very nature of God (2 Peter 1:4). Such participation in the life of God is an apt description of the work of the Holy Spirit. Through that sharing in God's nature, we grow in the Christian virtues that make our calling and election sure.

THE SPIRIT OF PROPHECY

The Holy Spirit was also intimately involved in producing the prophecies of Scripture. "Men spoke from God as they were carried along by the Holy Spirit" (2 Peter 1:21). Because we are confident of the Spirit's message, we can be certain of the truth of the story of

Jesus. That confidence guards us against those who would arrogantly pervert that story for their own personal power and greed.

The Spirit of Anticipation

Trust in the Spirit's voice also guards against impatience as we wait for the coming of the Lord. We wait for that coming through the Spirit who makes us spotless, blameless, and at peace. Through that Spirit we grow in grace and knowledge, we discern and guard against false teaching, and we speed the day when Jesus shall return

KNOW YOUR STORY

(2 Peter 1:1-21)

DAY ONE READING AND QUESTIONS

¹Simon Peter, a servant and apostle of Jesus Christ,

To those who through the righteousness of our God and Savior Jesus Christ have received a faith as precious as ours:

²Grace and peace be yours in abundance through the knowledge of God and of Jesus our Lord.

³His divine power has given us everything we need for life and godliness through our knowledge of him who called us by his own glory and goodness. ⁴Through these he has given us his very great and precious promises, so that through them you may participate in the divine nature and escape the corruption in the world caused by evil desires.

1. *Did the apostles and other eyewitnesses of Jesus have an advantage over later disciples like us? Was it easier for them to believe?*

2. *Do you feel as if God has given you all you need for life and godliness?*

3. *What are some of the precious promises God has given us?*

Day Two Reading and Questions

⁵For this very reason, make every effort to add to your faith goodness; and to goodness, knowledge; ⁶and to knowledge, self-control; and to self-control, perseverance; and to perseverance, godliness; ⁷and to godliness, brotherly kindness; and to brotherly kindness, love. ⁸For if you possess these qualities in increasing measure, they will keep you from being ineffective and unproductive in your knowledge of our Lord Jesus Christ. ⁹But if anyone does not have them, he is nearsighted and blind, and has forgotten that he has been cleansed from his past sins.

1. How do you react to the lists in the Bible? How should we react?

2. Which of these eight virtues that Peter discusses do you need most?

3. How does forgetting our forgiveness lead us to be unfruitful? Is this a call for guilt to motivate us?

Day Three Reading and Questions

¹⁰Therefore, my brothers, be all the more eager to make your calling and election sure. For if you do these things, you will never fall, ¹¹and you will receive a rich welcome into the eternal kingdom of our Lord and Savior Jesus Christ.

¹²So I will always remind you of these things, even though you know them and are firmly established in the truth you now have. ¹³I think it is right to refresh your memory as long as I live in the tent of this body, ¹⁴because I know that I will soon put it aside, as our Lord Jesus Christ has made clear to me. ¹⁵And I will make every effort to see that after my departure you will always be able to remember these things.

1. Do we still need to be reminded of the story of Jesus? Why, when we know it so well?

2. How do we make our calling and election sure? Does this imply we cannot be confident of our salvation?

3. What does Peter expect to happen to him soon? Does this change how we read his letter?

DAY FOUR READING AND QUESTIONS

[16]We did not follow cleverly invented stories when we told you about the power and coming of our Lord Jesus Christ, but we were eyewitnesses of his majesty. [17]For he received honor and glory from God the Father when the voice came to him from the Majestic Glory, saying, "This is my Son, whom I love; with him I am well pleased." [18]We ourselves heard this voice that came from heaven when we were with him on the sacred mountain.

[19]And we have the word of the prophets made more certain, and you will do well to pay attention to it, as to a light shining in a dark place, until the day dawns and the morning star rises in your hearts. [20]Above all, you must understand that no prophecy of Scripture came about by the prophet's own interpretation. [21]For prophecy never had its origin in the will of man, but men spoke from God as they were carried along by the Holy Spirit.

1. What event of Jesus' life does Peter claim to have eyewitnessed? What would it have been like to see that event?

2. Do you find some of the stories in the Bible unbelievable? Are they? Why do you believe?

3. How do Scripture, testimony, and experience combine to convince us the story of Jesus is true?

Day Five Reading and Questions

Go back and read the entire passage.

1. Is growing as a Christian our work or God's work?

2. Go back and list all the things God, Jesus, and the Holy Spirit do or will do for us in this passage.

3. Is Jesus the hero of your life story? Or do you think you are? What can we do to focus more on Jesus and less on ourselves?

MEDITATION ON 2 PETER 1:1-21

I had my eyes checked the other day, for the first time in four years. The optometrist surprised me by saying my glasses needed changing because my near-sightedness was improving! If I can only live to age 150 or so, I might be able to give up my glasses entirely!

But for the last thirty-five years (and for the foreseeable future) I have struggled with being short sighted. As annoying as that is, there is a deadlier form of short-sightedness. We can lose sight of what God has done for us in Christ. We can forget that he cleansed us from our sins. We can focus only on short-term pleasures and success, not on the distant glory with God.

Losing that focus on our past forgiveness and our future glory makes us blind to the calling of God. Blind to that marvelous story of Jesus. It is not a made-up story, but the climax of the story the prophets told—that God would send his dearly loved Son.

What happens when we are short-sighted? What happens when we forget our story? We fail to grow. Growth in Christ is not a way to earn all we need for life. Instead it is a seeing and remembering that

God has already given us all we need. It is growing into the story that we are God's beloved.

"Father, heal my blindness. Let me see your great love, shown in the story of Jesus."

MADE UP STORIES

(2 Peter 2:1-22)

DAY ONE READING AND QUESTIONS

¹But there were also false prophets among the people, just as there will be false teachers among you. They will secretly introduce destructive heresies, even denying the sovereign Lord who bought them—bringing swift destruction on themselves. ²Many will follow their shameful ways and will bring the way of truth into disrepute. ³In their greed these teachers will exploit you with stories they have made up. Their condemnation has long been hanging over them, and their destruction has not been sleeping.

1. *The false teachers deny Jesus. Do they do this openly? If not, how do they deny him?*

2. *Do all false teachers promise secret insight or knowledge? Give examples.*

3. *What is the contrast between made-up stories and the story Peter tells?*

DAY TWO READING AND QUESTIONS

⁴For if God did not spare angels when they sinned, but sent them to hell, putting them into gloomy dungeons to be held for judgment; ⁵if he did not spare the ancient world when he brought the flood

on its ungodly people, but protected Noah, a preacher of righteous-ness, and seven others; ⁶if he condemned the cities of Sodom and Gomorrah by burning them to ashes, and made them an example of what is going to happen to the ungodly; ⁷and if he rescued Lot, a righ-teous man, who was distressed by the filthy lives of lawless men ⁸(for that righteous man, living among them day after day, was tormented in his righteous soul by the lawless deeds he saw and heard)— ⁹if this is so, then the Lord knows how to rescue godly men from trials and to hold the unrighteous for the day of judgment, while continuing their punishment.¹⁰This is especially true of those who follow the corrupt desire of the sinful nature and despise authority.

> 1. *What do we know about fallen angels? Does this "knowledge" actu-ally come from the Bible? What other sources influence our thinking on angels?*

> 2. *What do the three Old Testament examples here have in common?*

> 3. *Whom does Peter give as an example of a righteous man among ungodly people? Does the Old Testament story of this man make him seem righteous? In what way is he righteous?*

Day Three Reading and Questions

Bold and arrogant, these men are not afraid to slander celes-tial beings; ¹¹yet even angels, although they are stronger and more powerful, do not bring slanderous accusations against such beings in the presence of the Lord. ¹²But these men blaspheme in matters they do not understand. They are like brute beasts, creatures of instinct, born only to be caught and destroyed, and like beasts they too will perish.

¹³They will be paid back with harm for the harm they have done. Their idea of pleasure is to carouse in broad daylight. They are blots

and blemishes, reveling in their pleasures while they feast with you. [14]With eyes full of adultery, they never stop sinning; they seduce the unstable; they are experts in greed—an accursed brood! [15]They have left the straight way and wandered off to follow the way of Balaam son of Beor, who loved the wages of wickedness. [16]But he was rebuked for his wrongdoing by a donkey—a beast without speech—who spoke with a man's voice and restrained the prophet's madness.

1. Whom do the false teachers slander? What does this mean?

2. What motivates the false teachers? Is that the motivation for many false teachers today?

3. What does it mean to be a beast? In what ways do the false teachers act less than human?

DAY FOUR READING AND QUESTIONS

[17]These men are springs without water and mists driven by a storm. Blackest darkness is reserved for them. [18]For they mouth empty, boastful words and, by appealing to the lustful desires of sinful human nature, they entice people who are just escaping from those who live in error. [19]They promise them freedom, while they themselves are slaves of depravity—for a man is a slave to whatever has mastered him. [20]If they have escaped the corruption of the world by knowing our Lord and Savior Jesus Christ and are again entangled in it and overcome, they are worse off at the end than they were at the beginning. [21]It would have been better for them not to have known the way of righteousness, than to have known it and then to turn their backs on the sacred command that was passed on to them. [22]Of them the proverbs are true: "A dog returns to its vomit," and, "A sow that is washed goes back to her wallowing in the mud."

1. What examples from nature does Peter use to describe the false teachers? What do those examples have in common?

2. What kind of freedom do the false teachers promise? How is that freedom actually slavery?

3. What two revolting animal examples does Peter use concerning the false teachers? Why is his language so disgusting?

DAY FIVE READING AND QUESTIONS

Go back and read the entire passage.

1. Have you known people who were accused of being false teachers who were innocent? How does this make you feel about all discussions of false teachers?

2. Are there false teachers today? If so, give examples. What do they teach?

3. Do all false teachers live false lives? Give examples.

MEDITATION ON 2 PETER 2:1-22

False prophets! False teachers! Heretics!

These words sound hollow in an age of tolerance. Surely none of us is right on all that we teach, unless we claim to know it all. We have been wrong before. So how can we condemn those who are wrong in their doctrine?

Because false teaching (in the biblical sense) always springs from false living. These "heretics" are not merely mistaken. They are intentionally deceiving others for the sake of money, pleasure, and power.

They sit at table with God's people—eating, laughing, and smiling—while all the time they are planning to cheat them.

No wonder they are compared o the worst characters in the Bible—fallen angels, Sodom, and Balaam. They act like brutes—ignorant, indulgent, and useless.

Why condemn these false teachers so strongly? Why warn of them so loudly? Because they threaten to enslave us. We need to remember that false teachers are not a thing of the past. They threaten us today. Promising freedom, they deceive us into bondage.

This is not an invitation to paranoia. The golden rule demands that we treat those who claim to be God's people as if they are, until they prove otherwise. But we dare not be naïve. There are some out there who will try to get our money and rule our lives through claims of power and holiness. How do we protect ourselves against such people? By knowing and living our story, the story of Jesus and his love.

"Lord Jesus, give me genuine love for my brothers and sisters. Guard me from those who would deceive me and deceive others."

THE DAY OF THE LORD

(2 Peter 3:1-18)

DAY ONE READING AND QUESTIONS

[1]Dear friends, this is now my second letter to you. I have written both of them as reminders to stimulate you to wholesome thinking. [2]I want you to recall the words spoken in the past by the holy prophets and the command given by our Lord and Savior through your apostles.

[3]First of all, you must understand that in the last days scoffers will come, scoffing and following their own evil desires. [4]They will say, "Where is this 'coming' he promised? Ever since our fathers died, everything goes on as it has since the beginning of creation."

1. How do the words of the prophets and of Jesus stimulate our wholesome thinking? Does this say something about the value of Bible study?

2. Why do some doubt the second coming?

3. What is a scoffer? Are scoffers still with us today?

DAY TWO READING AND QUESTIONS

[5]But they deliberately forget that long ago by God's word the heavens existed and the earth was formed out of water and by water. [6]By these waters also the world of that time was deluged and destroyed. [7]By the same word the present heavens and earth are

reserved for fire, being kept for the day of judgment and destruction of ungodly men.

⁸But do not forget this one thing, dear friends: With the Lord a day is like a thousand years, and a thousand years are like a day. ⁹The Lord is not slow in keeping his promise, as some understand slowness. He is patient with you, not wanting anyone to perish, but everyone to come to repentance.

1. Did those in Noah's day expect God to break into history in the flood? If they had, would they have lived differently? What does this say about living in expectation of the Second Coming?

2. What is a day like with the Lord? What does that mean?

3. What delays the Second Coming?

Day Three Reading and Questions

¹⁰But the day of the Lord will come like a thief. The heavens will disappear with a roar; the elements will be destroyed by fire, and the earth and everything in it will be laid bare.

¹¹Since everything will be destroyed in this way, what kind of people ought you to be? You ought to live holy and godly lives ¹²as you look forward to the day of God and speed its coming. That day will bring about the destruction of the heavens by fire, and the elements will melt in the heat. ¹³But in keeping with his promise we are looking forward to a new heaven and a new earth, the home of righteousness.

1. What will the day of the Lord come like? What does that mean?

2. If everything is to be destroyed, what value should we place on earthly things? Why do we spend so much time, money, and effort to gain possessions?

3. How do we speed the coming of Jesus?

DAY FOUR READING AND QUESTIONS

[14]So then, dear friends, since you are looking forward to this, make every effort to be found spotless, blameless and at peace with him. [15]Bear in mind that our Lord's patience means salvation, just as our dear brother Paul also wrote you with the wisdom that God gave him. [16]He writes the same way in all his letters, speaking in them of these matters. His letters contain some things that are hard to understand, which ignorant and unstable people distort, as they do the other Scriptures, to their own destruction.

[17]Therefore, dear friends, since you already know this, be on your guard so that you may not be carried away by the error of lawless men and fall from your secure position. [18]But grow in the grace and knowledge of our Lord and Savior Jesus Christ. To him be glory both now and forever! Amen.

1. Whose letters does Peter think are hard to understand? What does that say about our ability to see everything in the Bible alike?

2. Can Christians fall from grace? If so, how?

3. Isn't grace a gift? So, how do we grow in grace?

DAY FIVE READING AND QUESTIONS

Go back and read the entire passage.

1. Since it's been almost two thousand years since Christ went back to heaven, can we expect him as urgently as the first disciples did? Should we?

2. *When was the last time you thought about the Second Coming? Why?*

3. *How should we wait on the Second Coming?*

MEDITATION ON 2 PETER 3:1-18

Repent! The end is near! Get right or get left behind!

They sound like words we might see on a poster held high by a wild-eyed, long-bearded fanatic. The world has been around a long time. In every generation there have been some who are convinced the end was near. It wasn't. Jesus ascended almost 2000 year ago. It's been a long time. Whatever he meant when he said, "I'm coming soon," it does not seem that soon meant a matter of minutes or days or years or even centuries.

Can we really believe Jesus is coming again? Even in the first century, there were some who thought it had been a long time since he promised to return. Why is he waiting so long?

Peter gives three answers to that question. First, God is in control now as he was in the days of the flood. Second, God's time is not ours. If two thousand years is two days to God, then two days does not seem like long to wait. Third, Jesus delays his coming in order to give people time to turn to him. His tardiness is not due to apathy but out of patient concern.

How do we live in light of the Second Coming? I don't know if we can expect it today (although now would be a good time for it). But we can wait patiently by growing in the grace and knowledge of our Lord and Savior.

"Jesus, Lord and Savior, may I wait patiently for all things to be redeemed and transformed. Come quickly!"

THE LETTERS OF JOHN: THE SPIRIT OF LOVE

THE SPIRITUALITY OF THE LETTERS OF JOHN

These three brief letters interweave three major themes—love, truth, and knowledge. A healthy spirituality will thus deeply reflect the interplay of these three.

THE SPIRIT OF LOVE

God is love (1 John 4:8). He has lavished his love on us so that we should be called God's children. If we have this intimate relationship with God we live in love—love for him and for others. Loving others through acts of service is the sign that our love for God is genuine. We can be sure we live in this love because of the Spirit God has given us (1 John 3:24; 4:13). So, even though these letters never directly refer to the Holy Spirit as the Spirit of love, they make it clear that a genuine Christian spirituality is rooted in a visible sacrificial love for others and for God.

THE SPIRIT OF TRUTH

In these letters (as well as the rest of Scripture) truth is personal, not abstract. The Spirit of God in us acknowledges the truth that

Jesus came in the flesh (1 John 4:2-3). Since Jesus is the truth made flesh, then to acknowledge him is to be in the truth. What's more, the Spirit testifies to the truth of Jesus, The testimony of the Spirit is reliable because "the Spirit is the truth" (1 John 5:6). Thus the Spirit is the Spirit of Jesus, since both are spoken of as the truth. This truth lives deeply in our hearts, assuring us of the eternal life we have with God through his Son.

The Spirit of Knowledge

Truth and knowledge are obviously related. We know the truth because of the testimony of the Spirit in our hearts. We know that we are children of God and live in him because he has given us his Spirit (1 John 4:13). We also know what love is, because of what God has done for us. We know that love through the Spirit.

Therefore, these letters, written from a loving older Christian to his dear children in the faith, point us to a robust spirituality. The truly spiritual person is one who loves in deed, not just in word. Genuine spirituality never downplays truth, but knows the truth in person in Jesus and the Spirit. A healthy spirituality produces a confident knowledge of our standing before God, not based on what we have done, but on the actions and testimony of God in Christ through the Spirit. Let us listen to this call to a spirituality that loves, trusts, and knows the God of Truth.

LIFE, LIGHT, LOVE
(1 John 1:1-2:17)

DAY ONE READING AND QUESTIONS

¹That which was from the beginning, which we have heard, which we have seen with our eyes, which we have looked at and our hands have touched—this we proclaim concerning the Word of life. ²The life appeared; we have seen it and testify to it, and we proclaim to you the eternal life, which was with the Father and has appeared to us. ³We proclaim to you what we have seen and heard, so that you also may have fellowship with us. And our fellowship is with the Father and with his Son, Jesus Christ. ⁴We write this to make our joy complete.

1. Compare this passage with John 1:1-4. How are they similar?

2. What four "sense" words does John use to describe his experience of Jesus? In what ways have you "sensed" Jesus?

3. What does the word "fellowship" mean to you?

DAY TWO READING AND QUESTIONS

⁵This is the message we have heard from him and declare to you: God is light; in him there is no darkness at all. ⁶If we claim to have fellowship with him yet walk in the darkness, we lie and do not live by the truth. ⁷But if we walk in the light, as he is in the light, we have

fellowship with one another, and the blood of Jesus, his Son, purifies us from all sin.

[8]If we claim to be without sin, we deceive ourselves and the truth is not in us. [9]If we confess our sins, he is faithful and just and will forgive us our sins and purify us from all unrighteousness. [10]If we claim we have not sinned, we make him out to be a liar and his word has no place in our lives.

1. What does "God is light" mean? What do we associate with "light"?

2. What is the relationship between walking in the light and sin?

3. How does walking in light relate to forgiveness?

Day Three Reading and Questions

[1]My dear children, I write this to you so that you will not sin. But if anybody does sin, we have one who speaks to the Father in our defense—Jesus Christ, the Righteous One. [2]He is the atoning sacrifice for our sins, and not only for ours but also for the sins of the whole world.

[3]We know that we have come to know him if we obey his commands. [4]The man who says, "I know him," but does not do what he commands is a liar, and the truth is not in him. [5]But if anyone obeys his word, God's love is truly made complete in him. This is how we know we are in him: [6]Whoever claims to live in him must walk as Jesus did.

[7]Dear friends, I am not writing you a new command but an old one, which you have had since the beginning. This old command is the message you have heard. [8]Yet I am writing you a new command; its truth is seen in him and you, because the darkness is passing and the true light is already shining.

[9]Anyone who claims to be in the light but hates his brother is still in the darkness. [10]Whoever loves his brother lives in the light,

and there is nothing in him to make him stumble. [11]But whoever hates his brother is in the darkness and walks around in the darkness; he does not know where he is going, because the darkness has blinded him.

> 1. *For whom is Jesus the atoning sacrifice? What implications does that have?*

> 2. *How do we know that we have come to know Jesus?*

> 3. *Does John say he is writing an old command or a new one? What is that command? How is it both new and old?*

DAY FOUR READING AND QUESTIONS

[12]I write to you, dear children,
   because your sins have been forgiven on account of his name.
[13]I write to you, fathers,
   because you have known him who is from the beginning.
I write to you, young men,
   because you have overcome the evil one.
I write to you, dear children,
   because you have known the Father.
[14]I write to you, fathers,
   because you have known him who is from the beginning.
I write to you, young men,
   because you are strong,
   and the word of God lives in you,
   and you have overcome the evil one.
[15]Do not love the world or anything in the world. If anyone loves the world, the love of the Father is not in him. [16]For everything in the world—the cravings of sinful man, the lust of his eyes and the boasting of what he has and does—comes not from the Father but

from the world. [17]The world and its desires pass away, but the man who does the will of God lives forever.

1. *List the groups John writes to and the reason he writes each group. What quality is associated with older Christians ("fathers")? With younger Christians ("young men")?*

2. *What is the relationship between walking in the light and the world?*

3. *What three things does John say are "in the world?" Describe them in your own words.*

Day Five Reading and Questions

Go back and read the entire passage.

1. *Does this passage make you feel more certain of your salvation or less certain? Why?*

2. *Why does John constantly remind us not to sin? Is he trying to make us guilty? How does sin relate to assurance of salvation?*

3. *How do the three major themes of this passage—life, light, and love—intertwine?*

MEDITATION ON 1 JOHN 1:1-2:17

Fellowship. The word brings memories of church socials and potlucks, of punch and cookies. Fellowship always seemed to involve food and friends at our church.

But fellowship is a much deeper word. Bigger than simply time together with our Christian friends. Fellowship is sharing. Sharing money, time, pains, and joys. Fellowship is sharing our lives.

The letter of 1 John makes the word fellowship even deeper. Our fellowship is not simply with one another but with God himself. "And our fellowship is with the Father and with his Son, Jesus Christ" (1 John 1:3).

To have fellowship with God means we live in his light. It means we walk in the truth, walking as Jesus did (1 John 1:6). It means obedience to his commands. It means refusing the love of the world. It means the blood of Jesus continually cleanses us from sin. It means eternal life, the life of God.

But fellowship with God also means fellowship with his children. Through Christ, our relationships with fellow Christians are completely changed. They become more than mere human friendship (as wonderful as that can be). Instead all our relations to others are indirect; they are in Christ. That means we love our brothers and sisters, young and old, not because we have a great deal in common with them, but because we are made one in Christ.

Fellowship with God is, above all, a fellowship of love. God loves us through Christ. We love others through Christ. We live in a circle of unbroken love.

"God of love, may my love for you and for others be genuine, so I might fully enjoy fellowship with you and with them."

CHILDREN OF GOD

(1 John 2:18-3:24)

Day One Reading and Questions

[18]Dear children, this is the last hour; and as you have heard that the antichrist is coming, even now many antichrists have come. This is how we know it is the last hour. [19]They went out from us, but they did not really belong to us. For if they had belonged to us, they would have remained with us; but their going showed that none of them belonged to us.

[20]But you have an anointing from the Holy One, and all of you know the truth. [21]I do not write to you because you do not know the truth, but because you do know it and because no lie comes from the truth. [22]Who is the liar? It is the man who denies that Jesus is the Christ. Such a man is the antichrist—he denies the Father and the Son. [23]No one who denies the Son has the Father; whoever acknowledges the Son has the Father also.

[24]See that what you have heard from the beginning remains in you. If it does, you also will remain in the Son and in the Father. [25]And this is what he promised us—even eternal life.

[26]I am writing these things to you about those who are trying to lead you astray. [27]As for you, the anointing you received from him remains in you, and you do not need anyone to teach you. But as his anointing teaches you about all things and as that anointing is real, not counterfeit—just as it has taught you, remain in him.

1. What do most people think of the antichrist? How has Hollywood portrayed him? How does this passage describe him?

2. What is the anointing we have received from God? What does that anointing do for us?

3. What is truth in this passage?

DAY TWO READING AND QUESTIONS

²⁸And now, dear children, continue in him, so that when he appears we may be confident and unashamed before him at his coming.

²⁹If you know that he is righteous, you know that everyone who does what is right has been born of him.

¹How great is the love the Father has lavished on us, that we should be called children of God! And that is what we are! The reason the world does not know us is that it did not know him. ²Dear friends, now we are children of God, and what we will be has not yet been made known. But we know that when he appears, we shall be like him, for we shall see him as he is. ³Everyone who has this hope in him purifies himself, just as he is pure.

1. How does John want his readers to be at the coming of Jesus?

2. What does it mean to be children of God?

3. How are the children of God like Jesus? How will we be like him?

DAY THREE READING AND QUESTIONS

⁴Everyone who sins breaks the law; in fact, sin is lawlessness. ⁵But you know that he appeared so that he might take away our sins. And

in him is no sin. [6]No one who lives in him keeps on sinning. No one who continues to sin has either seen him or known him.

[7]Dear children, do not let anyone lead you astray. He who does what is right is righteous, just as he is righteous. [8]He who does what is sinful is of the devil, because the devil has been sinning from the beginning. The reason the Son of God appeared was to destroy the devil's work. [9]No one who is born of God will continue to sin, because God's seed remains in him; he cannot go on sinning, because he has been born of God. [10]This is how we know who the children of God are and who the children of the devil are: Anyone who does not do what is right is not a child of God; nor is anyone who does not love his brother.

1. Do Christians continue to sin?

2. What is the relationship between the Son of God and the devil?

3. How can one tell a child of God from a child of the devil?

Day Four Reading and Questions

[11]This is the message you heard from the beginning: We should love one another. [12]Do not be like Cain, who belonged to the evil one and murdered his brother. And why did he murder him? Because his own actions were evil and his brother's were righteous. [13]Do not be surprised, my brothers, if the world hates you. [14]We know that we have passed from death to life, because we love our brothers. Anyone who does not love remains in death. [15]Anyone who hates his brother is a murderer, and you know that no murderer has eternal life in him.

[16]This is how we know what love is: Jesus Christ laid down his life for us. And we ought to lay down our lives for our brothers. [17]If anyone has material possessions and sees his brother in need but has no pity on him, how can the love of God be in him? [18]Dear children, let us not love with words or tongue but with actions and in truth.

¹⁹This then is how we know that we belong to the truth, and how we set our hearts at rest in his presence ²⁰whenever our hearts condemn us. For God is greater than our hearts, and he knows everything.

²¹Dear friends, if our hearts do not condemn us, we have confidence before God ²²and receive from him anything we ask, because we obey his commands and do what pleases him. ²³And this is his command: to believe in the name of his Son, Jesus Christ, and to love one another as he commanded us. ²⁴Those who obey his commands live in him, and he in them. And this is how we know that he lives in us: We know it by the Spirit he gave us.

1. *What Old Testament example of not loving your brother does John give? Is this an extreme example, or do you know of those who hate their brothers ands sisters this much?*

2. *How do we know what love is?*

3. *How do we concretely show our love for others?*

Day Five Reading and Questions

Go back and read the entire passage.

1. *To be a child of God means we should act like God. According to this passage, how should we imitate God?*

2. *What does the Holy Spirit do for us in this passage?*

3. *How is Christian love for other Christians different from other types of love? What are some ways we express that love?*

MEDITATION ON 1 JOHN 2:18-3:24

"All your children shall be taught by the Lord" (Isaiah 54:13).

"But when he, the Spirit of truth, comes, he will guide you into all truth. He will not speak on his own; he will speak only what he hears, and he will tell you what is yet to come" (John 16:13).

"But you have an anointing from the Holy One, and all of you know the truth" (1 John 2:20).

What a joy it is to be taught by God through the anointing of the Holy Spirit! And what does that Holy Anointing teach us? It teaches what is sometimes so hard to grasp and believe.

We are children of God. That is what we are! Beloved children of the Almighty and All-Holy.

What does it mean to be God's children? It means when Jesus comes we will be like him. It means recognizing the antichrist in those who reject God's love in Jesus. It means living righteous lives that avoid sin. It means love of our brothers and sisters, love shown by acts of compassion.

The world conspires to convince us that we are not worthy to be called God's children. Voices outside us, sometimes from those who are closest to us, and voices inside our own heads repeatedly say, "Who are you kidding. You cannot be a child of God. You are too broken, too little, too sinful."

Those voices are wrong. The reason the world does not know us is that it did not know him. Only one truly knows us, and it is He who gives us the Holy Anointing that teaches us who we truly are.

We are God's children.

"Father, may I live this day confident that I am your beloved child. As your love enfolds me, may I spread my arms around those in need and show them your love."

GOD IS LOVE

(1 John 4:1-21)

DAY ONE READING AND QUESTIONS

[1]Dear friends, do not believe every spirit, but test the spirits to see whether they are from God, because many false prophets have gone out into the world. [2]This is how you can recognize the Spirit of God: Every spirit that acknowledges that Jesus Christ has come in the flesh is from God, [3]but every spirit that does not acknowledge Jesus is not from God. This is the spirit of the antichrist, which you have heard is coming and even now is already in the world.

[4]You, dear children, are from God and have overcome them, because the one who is in you is greater than the one who is in the world. [5]They are from the world and therefore speak from the viewpoint of the world, and the world listens to them. [6]We are from God, and whoever knows God listens to us; but whoever is not from God does not listen to us. This is how we recognize the Spirit of truth and the spirit of falsehood.

1. *How does one try the spirits? How can we recognize the Spirit of God?*

2. *If the one in us is greater than the one in the world, how should we live?*

3. *Are there false prophets today? Should we be afraid of them?*

Day Two Reading and Questions

⁷Dear friends, let us love one another, for love comes from God. Everyone who loves has been born of God and knows God. ⁸Whoever does not love does not know God, because God is love. ⁹This is how God showed his love among us: He sent his one and only Son into the world that we might live through him. ¹⁰This is love: not that we loved God, but that he loved us and sent his Son as an atoning sacrifice for our sins. ¹¹Dear friends, since God so loved us, we also ought to love one another. ¹²No one has ever seen God; but if we love one another, God lives in us and his love is made complete in us.

1. What does "God is love" mean? Does love completely describe God?

2. How did God show us what love is?

3. Why does John remind us that "no one has seen God?" What does this have to do with love?

Day Three Reading and Questions

¹³We know that we live in him and he in us, because he has given us of his Spirit. ¹⁴And we have seen and testify that the Father has sent his Son to be the Savior of the world. ¹⁵If anyone acknowledges that Jesus is the Son of God, God lives in him and he in God. ¹⁶And so we know and rely on the love God has for us.

God is love. Whoever lives in love lives in God, and God in him. ¹⁷In this way, love is made complete among us so that we will have confidence on the day of judgment, because in this world we are like him. ¹⁸There is no fear in love. But perfect love drives out fear, because fear has to do with punishment. The one who fears is not made perfect in love.

1. How do we know God lives in us?

2. How is fear the opposite of love?

3. What does perfect love do? How is this possible?

Day Four Reading and Questions

[19]We love because he first loved us. [20]If anyone says, "I love God," yet hates his brother, he is a liar. For anyone who does not love his brother, whom he has seen, cannot love God, whom he has not seen. [21]And he has given us this command: Whoever loves God must also love his brother.

1. If we say we love God, how should we treat a brother or a sister?

2. Are there those who claim to love God but hate their brothers and sisters? If so, give examples. How can those who hate others think they love God?

3. Why might we think it easier to love an unseen God than to love those people we do see?

Day Five Reading and Questions

Go back and read the entire passage.

1. What are some ways we use the word "love"? How does the idea that God is love change our definition of love?

2. Do you find it harder to love God or to love others? Why?

3. Is there a connection between false prophets, trying the spirits, and love?

MEDITATION ON 1 JOHN 4:1-21

How does one recognize God?

It seems like a simple question. How could one fail to recognize the Almighty? Yet there are many people who claim to speak for God, many voices clamoring for our attention. There are many who are more than willing to give us messages of comfort, therapy, and self-indulgence, justifying our worst impulses as the will of God.

How does one recognize God? How does one discern his voice? How does one test the spirits?

We know God because God is love. Where we see genuine love, there God is. And the greatest display of that measureless love of God is in Jesus Christ. That's why those who do not recognize Jesus do not know God. They have failed to see the depth of his love.

If we know God as love, then we live in faith, not fear. The one in us, the power of love, Love Himself, is stronger than the hatred in the world. Perfect love drives out fear—fear of the world and fear of punishment.

If we know the God of love, we love one another. We love with God's love, even doing good to those who hate us. Here is where our relationship with God is tested and proved genuine. It may seem easy to love a God whom we do not see. It's much harder to love real flesh-and-blood hard-to-get-along-with-people.

Who is it you find hard to love? Can you see God in them? Can you recognize him?

"God of love, pour your love into my heart this day through Jesus Christ and your Holy Spirit, so I might love the unlovable. May I be confident of your love toward unlovable me."

FAITH IN THE SON

(1 John 5:1-21)

DAY ONE READING AND QUESTIONS

¹Everyone who believes that Jesus is the Christ is born of God, and everyone who loves the father loves his child as well. ²This is how we know that we love the children of God: by loving God and carrying out his commands. ³This is love for God: to obey his commands. And his commands are not burdensome, ⁴for everyone born of God overcomes the world. This is the victory that has overcome the world, even our faith. ⁵Who is it that overcomes the world? Only he who believes that Jesus is the Son of God.

1. *What is the relationship between obedience and love? Do we normally associate obedience with love?*

2. *Do you ever feel as if the commands of God are burdensome? If so, why?*

3. *How does faith overcome the world? Give examples from your own life.*

DAY TWO READING AND QUESTIONS

⁶This is the one who came by water and blood—Jesus Christ. He did not come by water only, but by water and blood. And it is the Spirit who testifies, because the Spirit is the truth. ⁷For there are

three that testify: [8]the Spirit, the water and the blood; and the three are in agreement. [9]We accept man's testimony, but God's testimony is greater because it is the testimony of God, which he has given about his Son. [10]Anyone who believes in the Son of God has this testimony in his heart. Anyone who does not believe God has made him out to be a liar, because he has not believed the testimony God has given about his Son. [11]And this is the testimony: God has given us eternal life, and this life is in his Son. [12]He who has the Son has life; he who does not have the Son of God does not have life.

1. *Describe the three things that testify to us in our hearts.*

2. *What does it mean that Jesus came by water and blood?*

3. *What testimony has God given us? Is this testimony enough to create faith?*

Day Three Reading and Questions

[13]I write these things to you who believe in the name of the Son of God so that you may know that you have eternal life. [14]This is the confidence we have in approaching God: that if we ask anything according to his will, he hears us. [15]And if we know that he hears us— whatever we ask—we know that we have what we asked of him.

[16]If anyone sees his brother commit a sin that does not lead to death, he should pray and God will give him life. I refer to those whose sin does not lead to death. There is a sin that leads to death. I am not saying that he should pray about that. [17]All wrongdoing is sin, and there is sin that does not lead to death.

1. *Can we really know that we have eternal life? How?*

2. *What is the sin that leads to death? Is this similar to what Jesus calls the unpardonable sin?*

3. Why should we not pray for those whose sin is unto death? Shouldn't we pray for everyone?

Day Four Reading and Questions

[18]We know that anyone born of God does not continue to sin; the one who was born of God keeps him safe, and the evil one cannot harm him. [19]We know that we are children of God, and that the whole world is under the control of the evil one. [20]We know also that the Son of God has come and has given us understanding, so that we may know him who is true. And we are in him who is true—even in his Son Jesus Christ. He is the true God and eternal life.

[21]Dear children, keep yourselves from idols.

1. Do Christians sin? Do we continue to sin? What's the difference?

2. What is truth in these verses?

3. Does the last sentence seem like an abrupt end to this letter? Why do you think John ends the letter this way?

Day Five Reading and Questions

Go back and read the entire passage.

1. How are faith and love related in this chapter?

2. What is it we must believe? What is our faith in? Whom do we trust?

3. What is the relationship among faith, love, and sin? Why does John mention sin so much in a letter designed to assure us of salvation?

MEDITATION ON 1 JOHN 5:1-21

Obey. Keep the commands.

Such words frighten some of us. Is this not legalism? Can we keep the commands of God? After all, we have tried for years and can't seem to keep them all. If we do not obey perfectly, does that mean we really don't love God, no matter how much we say we do?

But John does not write to make us question our salvation but to assure us that we are children of God. He is not recommending a legalism that leads to despair. He only reminds us of what we all know. If we say we love God, we should listen to him and do what he says. He also reminds us that God's commands are never meant to be burdensome, but liberating. We are born of God and overcome the world!

So we show our love for God through obedience. That love and obedience is based on faith, not a foolish, blind faith, but one based on testimony. Water, blood, Jesus, Spirit, God—all give testimony that God has given us eternal life. We have this testimony in our hearts, and so we confidently approach God, knowing that he hears us. We pray for ourselves and our brothers and sisters who sin. God hears and gives life.

The choice is ours. We can trust, love, and obey the God who calls us his beloved children. Or we can give our love and put our faith in lesser goods and lesser gods. Keep away from idols! Serve Jesus Christ, the one true God and eternal life!

"Loving Father, may I obey you out of love, not out of fear, guilt, and shame. Give me faith in your testimony so I may trust that I have life in your Son."

THE TRUTH OF JESUS

(2 John)

DAY ONE READING AND QUESTIONS

[1]The elder,

To the chosen lady and her children, whom I love in the truth—and not I only, but also all who know the truth—[2]because of the truth, which lives in us and will be with us forever:

[3]Grace, mercy and peace from God the Father and from Jesus Christ, the Father's Son, will be with us in truth and love.

1. What does the author call himself? What does that mean?

2. If the lady he writes to is not a literal woman, who might she be?

3. We sometimes think Christians who love and Christians who have the truth are two different groups. Can one have truth and not love? Can one genuinely have Christian love and not have truth? What is the relationship between truth and love?

DAY TWO READING AND QUESTIONS

[4]It has given me great joy to find some of your children walking in the truth, just as the Father commanded us. [5]And now, dear lady, I am not writing you a new command but one we have had from the beginning. I ask that we love one another. [6]And this is love: that we walk in

obedience to his commands. As you have heard from the beginning, his command is that you walk in love.

   1. What is the relationship between love and obedience? Which is more important?

   2. Do we rejoice when others walk in the truth? Or are we secretly happy when we catch others in faults?

   3. Can you command love? What does this tell us about the biblical view of love as contrasted with the world's view?

DAY THREE READING AND QUESTIONS

[7]Many deceivers, who do not acknowledge Jesus Christ as coming in the flesh, have gone out into the world. Any such person is the deceiver and the antichrist. [8]Watch out that you do not lose what you have worked for, but that you may be rewarded fully. [9]Anyone who runs ahead and does not continue in the teaching of Christ does not have God; whoever continues in the teaching has both the Father and the Son.

   1. Who is the antichrist?

   2. What is the teaching of Christ?

   3. What can we do to keep from being deceived by false teachers?

DAY FOUR READING AND QUESTIONS

[10]If anyone comes to you and does not bring this teaching, do not take him into your house or welcome him. [11]Anyone who welcomes him shares in his wicked work.

¹²I have much to write to you, but I do not want to use paper and ink. Instead, I hope to visit you and talk with you face to face, so that our joy may be complete.

¹³The children of your chosen sister send their greetings.

1. *What should not be done for those who do not continue in the teaching of Christ? Is this being mean to them?*

2. *What is the difference between writing to Christian friends and seeing them face to face?*

3. *Who might the sister be who is mentioned here?*

DAY FIVE READING AND QUESTIONS

Go back and read the entire passage.

1. *Why is it important that Jesus came in the flesh? Would a spiritual incarnation not done just as well?*

2. *What is the relationship among truth, love, and obedience? Do we tend to separate these ideas and even put them against each other?*

3. *What is the overall tone of this short letter? Why does it sound that way?*

MEDITATION ON 2 JOHN

Many of us were raised in churches where truth was paramount. The truth (or our understanding of it) was used to bludgeon those who disagreed with us. They were not only mistaken, but they were false disciples who did not love the truth! As one preacher from my youth said, "Sometimes I think that my wife and I are the only ones left who follow the truth—and I'm not always sure about her!" I'm not sure he was kidding.

So talk of truth scares us. We prefer love to truth. We want to be loving, accepting people. We want our churches to be loving, warm places that embrace broken people. We do not want to beat them up with the truth, but bind their wounds with love.

But love and truth go together, says John. We love others in the truth. We walk in the truth, the great truth that we should love one another.

How can this be? How can truth (which seems so narrow and exclusive) and love (which seems so broad and accepting) come together in our lives? They meet in the flesh of Jesus. He is Truth, not abstract truth, but embodied truth. He is Love, not an easy love, but one that costs him his life.

How can we live in both truth and love? We live in Christ. We follow the teaching of Christ, which is Christ himself, the one who truly loves and lovingly teaches truth.

"Lord Jesus, you are the Truth. You are God who is Love. Fill me this day with your truth and love so I might truly love others."

FRIENDS FOR JESUS
(3 John)

Day One Reading and Questions

[1]The elder,

To my dear friend Gaius, whom I love in the truth.
[2]Dear friend, I pray that you may enjoy good health and that all may go well with you, even as your soul is getting along well. [3]It gave me great joy to have some brothers come and tell about your faithfulness to the truth and how you continue to walk in the truth. [4]I have no greater joy than to hear that my children are walking in the truth.

1. *What does the elder pray for concerning Gaius? Do we pray the same for our friends?*

2. *What does it mean for our souls to get along well? Do we often pray this for others?*

3. *When we hear that others are following the truth does it give us joy? Do we ever rejoice when others abandon the truth?*

Day Two Reading and Questions

[5]Dear friend, you are faithful in what you are doing for the brothers, even though they are strangers to you. [6]They have told the church about your love. You will do well to send them on their way in a manner worthy of God. [7]It was for the sake of the Name that they

went out, receiving no help from the pagans. [8]We ought therefore to show hospitality to such men so that we may work together for the truth.

  1. What is Gaius doing for the brothers?

  2. What are these brothers doing for the truth?

  3. What is hospitality? How do we show it today?

Day Three Reading and Questions

[9]I wrote to the church, but Diotrephes, who loves to be first, will have nothing to do with us. [10]So if I come, I will call attention to what he is doing, gossiping maliciously about us. Not satisfied with that, he refuses to welcome the brothers. He also stops those who want to do so and puts them out of the church.

  1. Do we love to be first? Why? How do we show that?

  2. Describe church leaders you have known who are like Diotrephes.

  3. Have you ever heard gossip about church leaders? Why do we gossip and listen to gossip about leaders of our church or other churches?

Day Four Reading and Questions

[11]Dear friend, do not imitate what is evil but what is good. Anyone who does what is good is from God. Anyone who does what is evil has not seen God. [12]Demetrius is well spoken of by everyone—and even by the truth itself. We also speak well of him, and you know that our testimony is true.

[13]I have much to write you, but I do not want to do so with pen and ink. [14]I hope to see you soon, and we will talk face to face.

Peace to you. The friends here send their greetings. Greet the friends there by name.

1. *"Anyone who does what is good is from God." Is this right? What does "good" mean here?*

2. *Contrast Demetrius with Diotrephes. Who do you know who is like Demetrius?*

3. *Truth itself speaks well of Demetrius. What does that mean? How does truth speak?*

DAY FIVE READING AND QUESTIONS

Go back and read the entire passage.

1. *Should leaders help themselves or help others? Do we associate leadership with self-promotion? Should we?*

2. *In this letter is truth simply something to believe or something to do? How do we do the truth?*

3. *How do we help missionaries? How should we help them?*

MEDITATION ON 3 JOHN

What does it mean to be a friend? Usually it means that we are friendly with those who like us and are our friends.

But spiritual friendship is much more. It means caring about the spiritual health of our friends as much (or more) than we care about their physical health. It means walking with another in the truth. It even means caring for strangers, showing hospitality to our brothers and sisters.

The opposite of this spiritual friendship is seen in Diotrephes, "who loves to be first." That "me-first" attitude shows itself in lack of hospitality, malicious gossip, and excluding others from the church.

By contrast, Demetrius is well spoken of by all, even the truth itself. His kind of spiritual friendship is an example to all.

"Lord Jesus, as you welcomed all, even sinners, so may I show genuine hospitality in your name. Keep me from selfish pride."

JUDE: DENYING JESUS

The Spirituality of Jude

It seems strange to even search for spirituality in a letter that focuses on the errors and fate of false teachers. Condemning heresy does not seem spiritual! But if we understand that these false teachers are intentionally leading people away from the grace found in Jesus, then opposing them is a spiritual act. What's more, Jude shows that the greatest defense against false teaching is to focus on faith, pray in the Spirit, keep ourselves in God's love, and wait for the mercy of Jesus. Thus, this brief and neglected letter points us to life in the Spirit as a shield against those who would deceive us.

DAY ONE READING AND QUESTIONS

[1]Jude, a servant of Jesus Christ and a brother of James,
To those who have been called, who are loved by God the Father and kept by Jesus Christ:
[2]Mercy, peace and love be yours in abundance.
[3]Dear friends, although I was very eager to write to you about the salvation we share, I felt I had to write and urge you to contend for the faith that was once for all entrusted to the saints. [4]For certain men whose condemnation was written about long ago have secretly slipped in among you. They are godless men, who change the grace of our God into a license for immorality and deny Jesus Christ our only Sovereign and Lord.

1. If Jude had written about the salvation we share, what would that letter have been like?

2. What does it mean to contend for the faith? How do we do this?

3. How can grace become a license for immorality? Can this be done today? How can we prevent this?

DAY TWO READING AND QUESTIONS

[5]Though you already know all this, I want to remind you that the Lord delivered his people out of Egypt, but later destroyed those who did not believe. [6]And the angels who did not keep their positions of authority but abandoned their own home—these he has kept in darkness, bound with everlasting chains for judgment on the great Day. [7]In a similar way, Sodom and Gomorrah and the surrounding towns gave themselves up to sexual immorality and perversion. They serve as an example of those who suffer the punishment of eternal fire.

[8]In the very same way, these dreamers pollute their own bodies, reject authority and slander celestial beings. [9]But even the archangel Michael, when he was disputing with the devil about the body of Moses, did not dare to bring a slanderous accusation against him, but said, "The Lord rebuke you!" [10]Yet these men speak abusively against whatever they do not understand; and what things they do understand by instinct, like unreasoning animals—these are the very things that destroy them.

[11]Woe to them! They have taken the way of Cain; they have rushed for profit into Balaam's error; they have been destroyed in Korah's rebellion.

1. What three examples of disobedience and punishment does Jude give from the Old Testament in verses 5-7? What do those three have in common?

2. What is it these false teachers do not understand? How do they show their lack of understanding?

3. What three examples of disobedience and punishment does Jude give from the Old Testament in verse 11? What do those three have in common?

DAY THREE READING AND QUESTIONS

¹²These men are blemishes at your love feasts, eating with you without the slightest qualm—shepherds who feed only themselves. They are clouds without rain, blown along by the wind; autumn trees, without fruit and uprooted—twice dead. ¹³They are wild waves of the sea, foaming up their shame; wandering stars, for whom blackest darkness has been reserved forever.

¹⁴Enoch, the seventh from Adam, prophesied about these men: "See, the Lord is coming with thousands upon thousands of his holy ones ¹⁵to judge everyone, and to convict all the ungodly of all the ungodly acts they have done in the ungodly way, and of all the harsh words ungodly sinners have spoken against him." ¹⁶These men are grumblers and faultfinders; they follow their own evil desires; they boast about themselves and flatter others for their own advantage.

¹⁷But, dear friends, remember what the apostles of our Lord Jesus Christ foretold. ¹⁸They said to you, "In the last times there will be scoffers who will follow their own ungodly desires." ¹⁹These are the men who divide you, who follow mere natural instincts and do not have the Spirit.

1. Jude compares the false teachers to what three examples from nature? What do these have in common?

2. What word does Enoch and Jude use most often to describe these false teachers? What does that say about them?

3. *Why does Jude mention what the apostles said? Are false teachers a new, unexpected occurrence?*

Day Four Reading and Questions

[20]But you, dear friends, build yourselves up in your most holy faith and pray in the Holy Spirit. [21]Keep yourselves in God's love as you wait for the mercy of our Lord Jesus Christ to bring you to eternal life. [22]Be merciful to those who doubt; [23]snatch others from the fire and save them; to others show mercy, mixed with fear—hating even the clothing stained by corrupted flesh.

[24]To him who is able to keep you from falling and to present you before his glorious presence without fault and with great joy— [25]to the only God our Savior be glory, majesty, power and authority, through Jesus Christ our Lord, before all ages, now and forevermore! Amen.

1. *What does it mean to pray in the Holy Spirit? How does such prayer build our faith and fight false teachers?*

2. *Should we show mercy to false teachers? To whom should we show mercy? How?*

3. *What is the point of the song of praise at the end of this letter? Why do you think Jude ended the letter this way?*

Day Five Reading and Questions

Go back and read the entire passage.

1. *Name some false teaching around today. Does that teaching threaten God's people? How do we fight it?*

2. *What attitude should we have as we fight false teaching? What attitudes must we avoid? Is it possible to be right in your teaching but wrong in the way you defend it?*

3. *Who is it that ultimately protects us from falling into false teaching? How do we rely on him?*

MEDITATION ON JUDE

There are many ways to deny Jesus. One might simply deny that he is the Son of God. One might deny him through neglect, never really considering who he is. Most dangerous and subtle are those who claim to follow Jesus, even claim to know him better than others, but who deny him by the way they live.

So it is that false teachings in the Bible are always false "livers." That is, they are not merely wrong about Jesus but they intentionally lead others away from him through their immoral lives. Here lies the danger of false teachers, not that they are sincerely mistaken, but that they take advantage of others, gaining money and influence through deception.

So how should we fight false teaching? Not by using the weapons of the false teachers—arrogance, deception, and power—but by remembering what we were taught and who we are. We were taught the way of Jesus. We trust in him. We are those who have the Spirit and so we pray in the Spirit. We are loved by God, and that is the basis of the mercy we receive. We also fight for the faith by showing mercy, not hatred, to others.

Most of all, we continue to trust the only one who is able to keep us from falling—the only God, our Savior.

"God, my Savior, through the Holy Spirit I pray that you will strengthen my faith in Jesus Christ, my Lord. Keep me from any teaching and practice that would deny him."

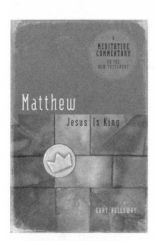
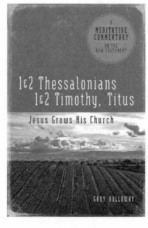
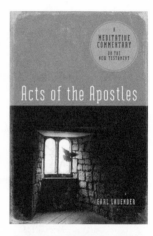
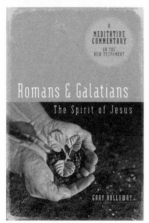
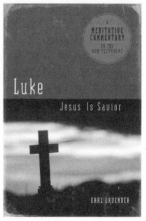